zen telegrams

Zen

79 picture poems

rutland vermont : tokyo japan :

by paul reps

charles e. tuttle company

Representatives

For Continental Europe:
BOXERBOOKS, INC., Zurich

For the British Isles:
PRENTICE-HALL INTERNATIONAL, INC., London

For Australasia:
PAUL FLESCH & CO., PTY. LTD., Melbourne

For Canada:
M. G. HURTIG LTD., Edmonton

Published by the Charles E. Tuttle Company, Inc.
of Rutland, Vermont & Tokyo, Japan
with editorial offices at
Suido 1-chome, 2-6, Bunkyo-ku, Tokyo

Library of Congress Catalog Card No. 59-8189

International Standard Book No. 0-8048-0645-4

First edition, 1959

First paper-bound edition, 1962

Tenth printing, 1971

Printed in Japan

table of contents

1

2

3

editor's foreword

a book, like a life, must have a name. When Reps has to give a name to his picture-poems, he generally calls them "poems before words." But when I come to collect them into this book, I have chosen to call them "Zen telegrams."

Reps never has labeled his picture-poems as Zen. "Zen," he has commented, "is a word I now almost never use. It is for children, for those innocent." Here he is speaking, and nowise disparagingly, of Zen as a formalized religion, a way of Buddhism that seeks--through "quiet sitting," meditation-- the sudden flash of self-enlightenment that sets man free of earthly limitations, free of the need of words. But the word Zen has also taken on a wider meaning in recent years and is now often applied to a certain way of thinking, of aesthetics, of living. Reps himself has said: "Zen, cryptic as 'jazz,' is now a world word for God or Buddha in us shaking us alive after we've asked for it, earned it."

So it has seemed to me that his picture-poems glow with the unmistakable light that, for lack of a better word, may be most immediately described as this wider-meaning Zen. Certainly the label serves pointedly to say these picture-poems are akin to the Zen koan, to the shining instant the Zen masters evoked with these nonsensical conundrums that often made more "sense" than a library of philosophy. When Reps remarks that "poems before words intend to let the seer invite his originative life rhythm rather than having it imposed upon him," is he not saying Zen? is he not speaking as a long-time Zen familiar?

As for "telegrams," I have occasionally heard him call his picture-poems so. To me this seems exactly the word needed--both common enough and yet sharp enough to describe these communications that in intent are more than pictures, more than poems. If Zen is old, telegrams are very much of today. The juxtaposition of the two words points, then, to both the immediacy and the datelessness of what's here. If Zen works as a flash of insight, so do these. They do so telegraphically, freshly; they are not cast in the gone past. Who can resist opening a telegram?

When I once told him how much I liked a certain one of his pictures, Reps replied: "Tell me about the words, not the ink shapes!" For, as he has explained, the "ink shapes" are not for themselves but for giving another dimension to the words. In a sense, then, he is trying, through the medium of these shapes, to give the English word some of that pictorial, flashing quality which the ideographs of China and Japan possess in their own right, the quality that breathes magical life into their calligraphy. "Black brush lines on white space, such as calligraphy," he has observed, "are treasured by the Chinese and Japanese, who feel they receive something of the writer through them. They do not call them art. It is something from the heart."

And again: "Their calligraphy is picture writing. The character for man 人 pictures a man, field 田 looks like a field, and river 川 shows as well as says river. 人 田 川 becomes a three-picture poem, with each individual supplying his own detail and interpretation. Since eighty-five percent of our sensing comes through our seeing, picturing is primal poeming. With an alphabet language we are left straining to see, but not seeing, one step removed from the delight of a picturing way of thinking. Pictures are before words, in them, inclusive of them. Poems before words would see-say in this same care-less way and thus dip into primal vitality."

Reps first started creating his picture-poems in Japan in 1952, using them as what he calls "weightless gifts" and scattering them among his many friends, old and always new, as he moved about the world. In 1957 a Japanese poet friend to whom he had given a number of them started the first of the Reps picture-poem shows. In this Kyoto exhibit, as in all later ones, the poems, on rice paper of various sizes, were scotch-taped only at the tops to horizontal bamboo poles strung from the ceiling at different levels, and electric fans were made to blow them gently. There they fluttered like washing in the breeze, and the scene had somewhat the appearance of moving banners. There was also a sign that read:

> 1,000 yen each to automobile-owners
> 500 yen to well-dressed persons
> 200 yen to students
> 100 yen to anyone poor
> 10 yen to lovers of Buddha

"No one elected to pay ten yen," someone has observed, "so perhaps each loved himself more than Buddha." But thousands came to "read-see" and many

11

stayed long. Each always seemed to find some particular one he liked for his own reasons, and Reps would give it to him or sell it at the price the buyer chose, and then draw another to hang in its place, sometimes the same one, sometimes a new one.

After that, Osaka wanted a show, then Tokyo, then Kyoto again--and now I hear talk of Washington, Honolulu, Rome. The picture-poems were televised, newsreeled, radioed, written about, and even reproduced on silken obi in microscopic stitches of silk for elegant ladies. And his creating of the poems still continues, so that I've found myself with almost two hundred to choose from. To fit the space, I've had to winnow these down to seventy-nine, arranging them in four sections of sixteen each and one section of fifteen. The titles given in the table of contents are not formal titles but only key words that I've found convenient as memory aids.

Seventy-nine poems? "No," comments Reps, speaking both to me and to future readers of this book, "actually there's only one poem, and that one too a weightless gift. Any one is for one person. Like intimate conversation, it is not meant to be seen-heard by others. All this writing and exhibiting and publishing may seem far from 'one for one'--or as near as you let it be. Perhaps then, only perhaps, one of these is for you. Should this be so, you are welcome to take it out of the book and hang it on your wall, knowing it was done for you with delight."

Meredith Weatherby

Stop

innocently
joy   is

15

pine drinking
luminous dew
as if nothing
had happened

potato
seeing
everywhere
below

and
glistening
wisps
of
straw

Living earth to comfort
Living water to heal
Living air   purify
radiance   reveal

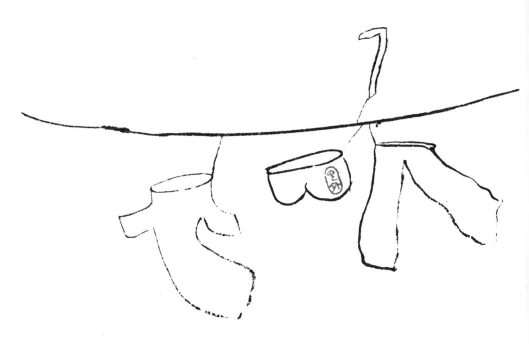

washing
dancing
hurry

19

though
wide the sky
never lost
wild geese
        cry

sometimes
in may rain
I can hear
my fingernails.
growing

brookside
          alive
o do not hasten
               friend
you may arrive

below

ever

above

now
now

cobwebs
hesitating
us

SOFtLy
teLLing hand
to open

———————————/——————

SoFtly

hand

opens

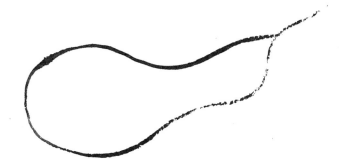

cucumber
unaccountably
cucumbering

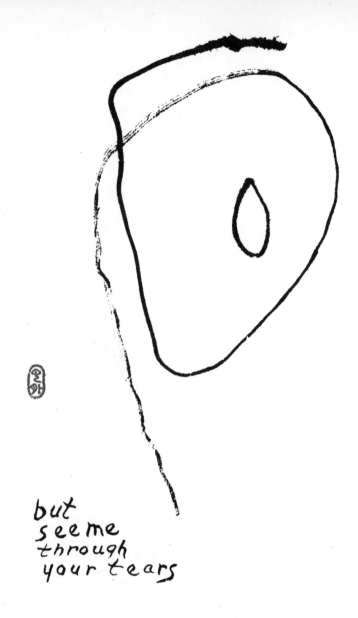

but
see me
through
your tears

words
unsaid

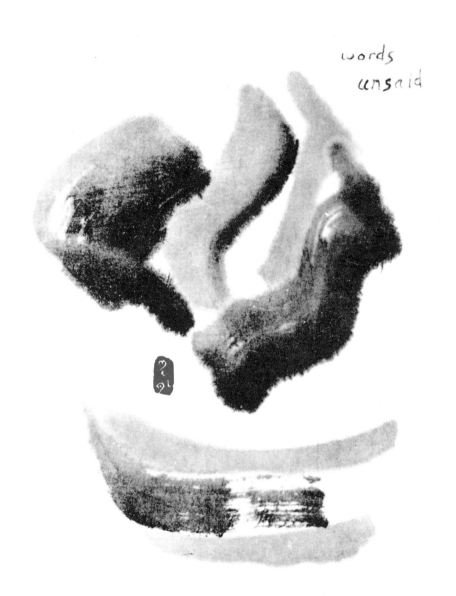

under my
clothes
I am naked
too

please
telephone me
in the
ricefield

who
is

shrieking
torn from
stem
the flower

well
silently
overflowing

seeing the smile
in your eyes
I have forgotten
that people die

after 50,000 years
rapturous in sky
I find you
        living
            in a box

38

who can say
I am Japanese
    american
        African
  when in the next day
    he may be a butterFLy

39

already
weeds
are writing
the scriptures

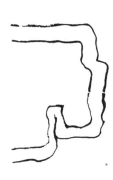

earthworm
writing Letters
to mankind

world through
        my door
    how wide
house how tiny
    From outside

lose your
un-Flower
mind

43

suddenly
from tree
peach blossom
how can this be

use us
the bamboo
whisper

period
comma
sunset

drinking
a bowl of green tea
I stopped the war

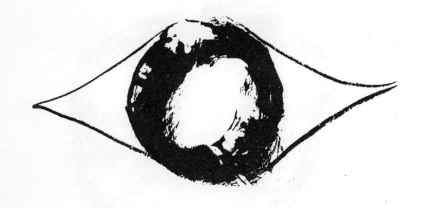

sun
between
Fingers

reps

holding sun
into Forehead
sages became
men oF Light

48

Laughing
I
makes
a tree

do not
step
on our
tears

Face
in
Face

black resting
white transforming

53

consciousness
deLighting
as crane

grain of
sand
spins
round

child
too

turtle
explaining
don't act
but act

silently
the river
silently

Fighting wrens
   isn't there room
   enough in this world

58

walking
between
the raindrops

59

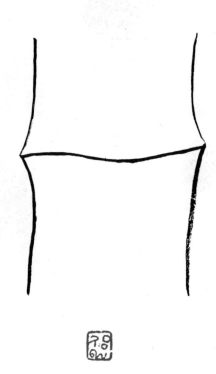

sound of flute
has returned
to bamboo
      forest

moth caressing
my cheek
may be you

giant redwood
in-tellingly
compressing
into a seed

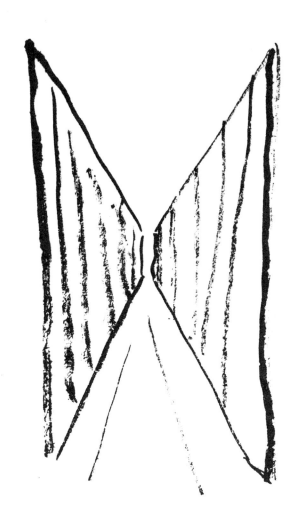

even downtown
surrendering
my breath

born
yet unborningly
reeds

ants
how thankFul
I am
with no thing
to be thankFul
For

forgotten
string
sings

66

upon
Fallen
Leaves

a

Leaf

let   moss   be   moss

69

5-stone
garden

drop stones
  unexpectedly
    From closed hand
      see the garden you

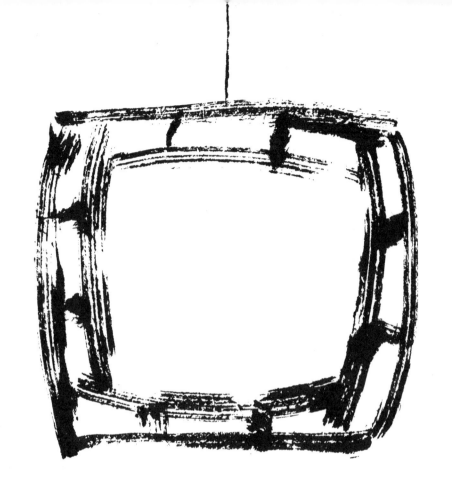

square wheel
to go backwards

move in
unheard
music

dust
of
dust
of
must

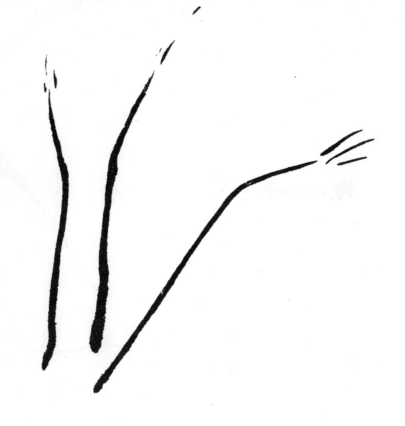

which
weed
am I

ah
Farmer Food
herbs
brown rice
greens
sprouts
a Farmer
wife

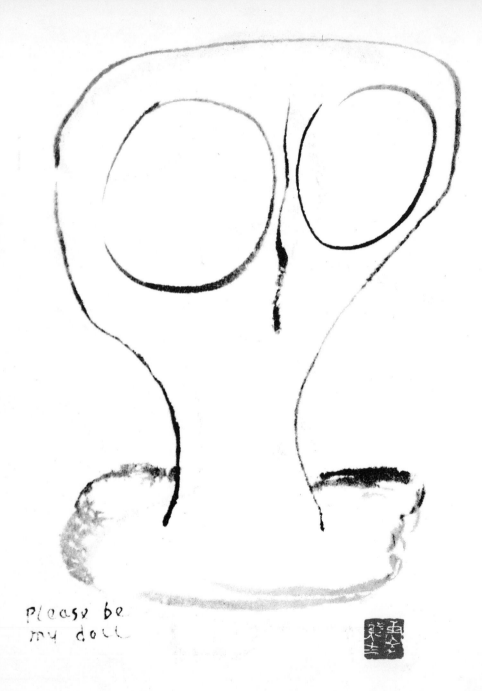

please be
my doll

76

my life
as path
of fish

until
you
cry

no

78

IF OF me
a picture
you a picture
take

don't worry
day
will come

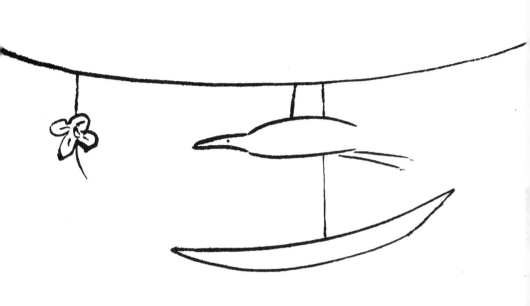

paper flower
paper bird
paper moon

who walks
the wild earth
any more?

Since men
    still make war
Let me lie down and sing
    with the grasses

rocks preaching
Become some
Silent
sound

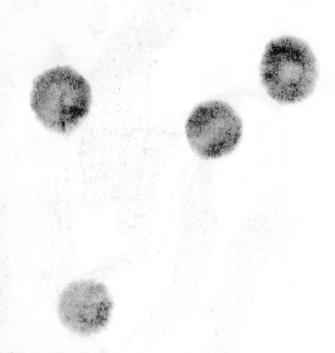

perhaps only
          perhaps
   you stand beside me
    in the gentle rain

84

9

Little bud
open this heart
with your
invisible hands

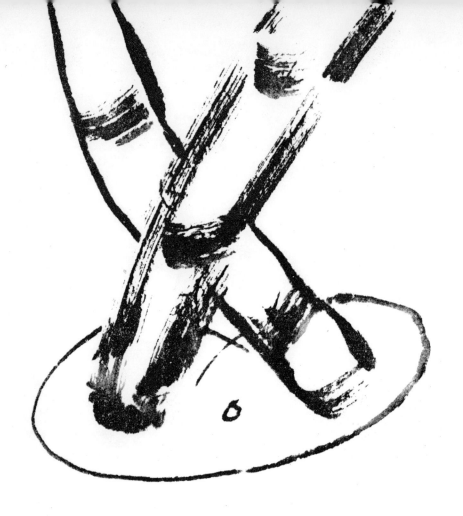

pebble
receiving
Love

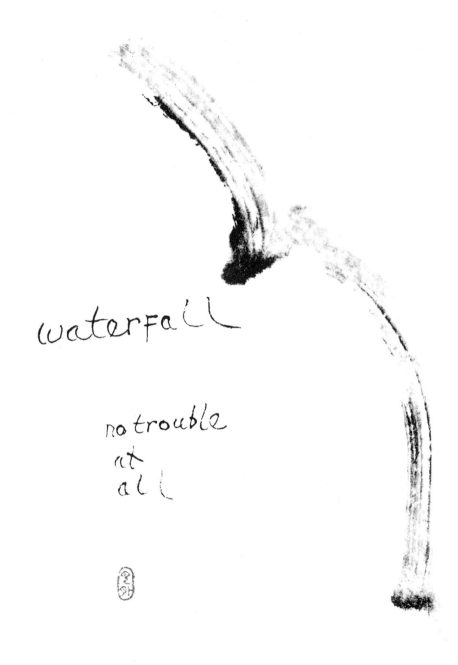

waterfall

no trouble
at
all

now that
everybody's in
a hurry
let's ride your
bicycle
through the
ricefields

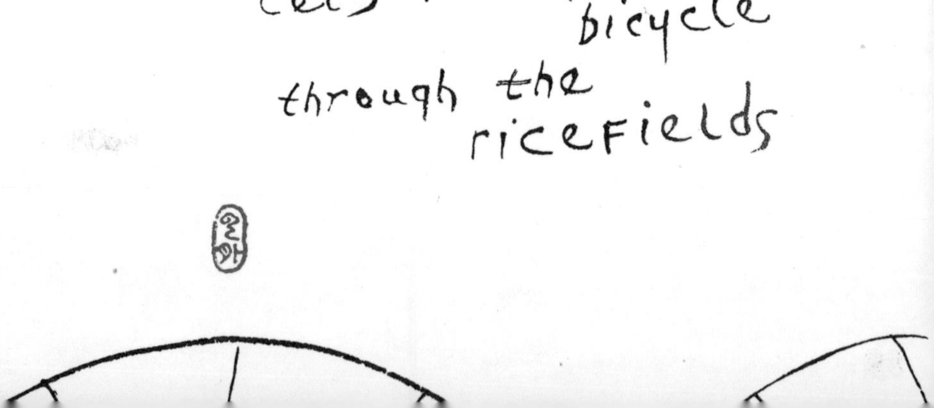

2nd-hand. words climbing a thread

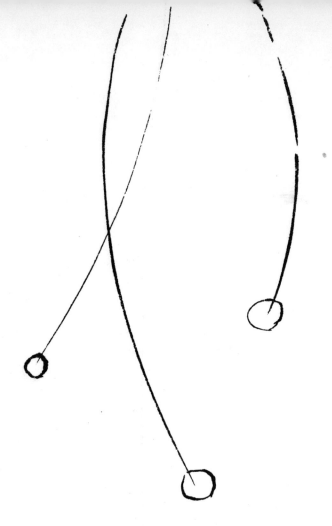

captured
snowflakes
suffering

snow

if only
I could tell
you my name
tomorrow

mountain
rising lines
to center
sudden
Light

asking
seed how to open
roots how to grow:
"open"   "grow"

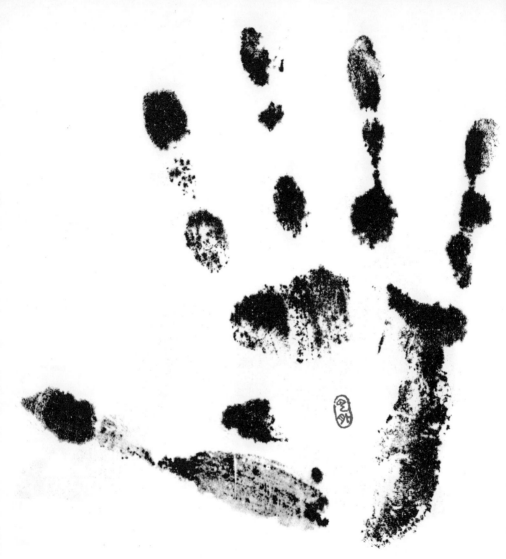

Buddha compassion
Jesus Love
and touch of a hand

cut some humans from their stems
tie them in a bunch
pull a few out
stick them in a vase
look at them

throw
the
rest
away

Human arrangement
by Flowers

something

something

nothing

nothing

98

in her
tender
unfathomable
being

how to
be
a
samurai

SUN FELL
on me